Get up eight

Patrick Williamson

Acknowledgments

The following poems or versions thereof have been published as follows:

January Review
Lightly, lightly

Cooch Behar
Become silent

Noon: journal of the short poem
Loneliness

Lothlorien
No fixed abode, Snowfall, Looking, Spring beauties

The Antonym
May

The World into Words
Sacred place

Ink, Sweat & Tears
The temple at nightfall, The 7.14

Doublespeak
In flight, Cross-legged

Vital Spark
–/—//—

La Traductière
It all seems so simple

The Fortnightly Review
All notes lead here, Moon-time

Words for the wild
The Glosters return

New Contexts 5
Those that witness

NiftyLit
October in Bucharest

World Poetry Tree
Looking

Beach Hut
The shoreline

Osiris
Sea and land

International Times
Are you listening?, Subterranean explorers of words

Contents

Lightly, lightly

Sometimes I'm thinking without thoughts.

It's not the mind's a blank, just
I only sense the body's sounds, and texture,
if you see what I mean.

Often when I can't sleep
or during a mid-afternoon lull, after a nap
on Sunday usually.

It's as if I'm looking for the next step or line,
but nothing is taking shape.
I just have to decide what to do with time ahead.

The episode passes, duly noted.
It's because I'm trying too hard,
must learn to do everything lightly.

Become silent

coil up in our roots, fragile in this darkness,
seeking out meetings, I am so close,
your hands combing the hair of solitude

nurse always replies not yet, I am so far,
the winds dare embroil sky and earth,
here I better to settle the agitated waves

she often asks, when am I leaving,
you can't walk well, visits are end-of-life,
yet it befits us to gain this battle

make the moment count, no matter,
how I long for some-one here to arrive
I can't tell you, how many times I

Loneliness

I have been careful not to admit it.
I rely on its syllables.
I await.

Meeting

My brother's hair
is thinning

and turning a fine white
like my father's,

days later I understand
part of the anxiety

that wakes me at night
is this sense of mortality

reminded of then,
no matter who we are,

and he spoke of
preparation

on earth as in heaven.

Companion

You really wonder, it seems such
an easy task, to take you there,
while watching your back, who knows

what lies ahead, we'll get at the end.
I trust you in this, as always.
In the forest, deep in the thickets.

I didn't understand what you said.
Don't be silly, that's just a ford,
we'll cross it easily, make a splash.

No fixed abode

I imagine that care, patience & desperation,
left for posterity in these photographs
brought to life by my father's voice, his memory;
stacked in your posthumous attic room.

This life carted over borders, across Irish lands
& the Apennines; we glimpse your days
in black & white, that summer before the war
my father smoking, sipping tea on the terrace.

This suitcase life, that elusive house sought
but never found, days circled, solitude
dragged along, then this crumbled earth damp
to touch, your voice forever still.

May

One will have to yield without groaning
and crumple under the bluish roots

what will I say to the pebbles and carefree bark
that they don't already know

be sure of May foliage and its songs
let my lips feel the kisses of an absent lover

with night so careful to watch closely
the edge of the sheet, its hospital corners,

as the dream of sun and chatter dies down,
there's fresh-cut flowers, she thought

he's caressing me again, but neither breath
nor heat was, he hadn't even groaned.

Snowfall

There's a bloke spreads grit in early morning,
a train passing in a haze of blown snow,
an unknown outline that appears, trembling glass

a girl who films herself, the leap to tarmac;
this whispered whine of wind among leaves
the lament of a body tumbling in dim light,

dark strands swaying in a pool of blindness
brush flakes that touch a cheek, on the verge,
to be human and understand is not enough.

Looking

Suddenly I was left searching for the future
     I kept this bottle, green pot and packet of spice
as a souvenir of those days,
leaving behind twilight for the tongue of hope.

Suddenly there is quiet, after the rush to catch that last train,
     I retain the beauty of your simple movements,
     I kneel among fluted columns, hiding thoughts in shadow.

Our shoulders hunched, late at night,
     the spread of ink scrolled on, learning,
at work, we shared evening time, passing time, love.

Spring beauties

The fine faces of your riotous fellows,
their thick brogue, remind me –

coffee dear Alan in the cloister café
both wildly exclaiming Italian –

sparrows, perched on railings, pecking
for crumbs from scones, the wind strong –

I'm taking pictures of the cathedral cross,
blue-black in the civil twilight –

bronze-throated cream beauties enfold us,
shields, sun raying from the centre

and outer rings of life, to chase the enemy
make rain in periods of drought.

That old photo I found

This walk stretches along bustling streets
these walls are light yellow and ochre,

we strode around for years, suspecting
there was more to it, we joined forces

to send these old blurry images back
as a radiating raised-sun surrounded us

its patterns moving toward the edge
equidistant, tapering golden bodies,

our hunch was correct, there was more to this,
the moon still shining behind rays of trees.

Salt and smokes

Boxes of salt are stacked by the door
the Romans had a state monopoly,

let me try the super-lottery again, maybe,
as I return, you exit, clutching packets,

blow rings around me, later I try hard to
look assured at this evening's event,

photographers retreating before VIPs,
flash-bulbs and Instagram, the roads

smoothed here, the rest of world rocky,
pot-holed, graffitied twisting flyovers,

all of which so detached, so hard to spark
into life, yet sun still bathes our room,

balm for crevassed skin, welcome respite,
we didn't win, but there's always salt.

Sacred place

bank and fall undercloud, leave

light breaks into discordances
above the surface horizon, deep

the air and dark, substantial,
black, you pierce it as with a wedge

the sun sets on one side, puff
forest the other, rainland often

shafting flight that frees glances

do not make me that blind statue,
that intrusion of space waiting

what's sacred about place,
what we bring there, consolation,

hope, whatever the morning brings,
essential strength in

this perplexing time.

Exodus

Seek refuge from burning forest,
pitch-steaming men, life limb in peril,

flee the wildfires of shores, rages
of the world, such displacing events

thrust you over wildfires of the sea,
storms stirring, to rift the last refugia,

we swarm to these pockets but
insect predators got to first,

so find solace in evening *Anemoi,*
eyes meeting eyes, picture-perfect

not, but a presence that shall stay
with you, and give you rest.

The temple at nightfall

We link arms down the aisles
        of the peristyle, sunset walk
in this adyton of ours, mull
        life's paradoxes, as salt-spray
blows in under antefixes, as
        the ocean rolls with mysteries
we listen to the ebb and swell
        each wave another lungful,
the love that wells behind
        heaving ribs, searching
for breath but the water
        keeps rising no
matter what draining can do,
        while your eyes always
look out to the porticos,
        the horizon, without fail.

Frescoes

Instead of seeing in these figures
the evocation of another life
one should see a remembrance,
an initiation in mystery, purifying

as the covering lid is raised,
waning sunlight floods inside,
brings these marvels to life
after millennia in the coldness,

for the kingdom of the dead
is the world of silence, so
the question remains then,
what did the frescoes mean?

Creators

splatter and shape,
        bracket the spirit, rib
worlds in ether, erect a backbone
        for us spineless drifters, let
them be wise and sententious

meaningfully engaged,
        you know, on this journey of
substance and absence, which
        draws on personal narrative,
inner reaches of our state

a man's soul lies naked there,
        what passes within
undisguised in its natural process,
        you see systems and motives
the same heart, this evidence,
        interdependence of being.

In flight

the snow-capped is a plosive
landscape of shards of flint
uncomfortable for giant fakirs
to tread, valleys are animal backs
feeding at the rack, valleys a whisp,
fathomless smoking sunlight,
climb to the crest, traverse this,
icing-sugar slopes are mortal
seamless frontiers staunch sieves,
the blue light reveals a death

in flight.

–/—//—

They arrive, a tardy, em, dash
to chisel en another fashion
fragments, insert a network core
to stop these pipes knocking
each other down, and they fling
straining sacks into a void -
for we lack joints, cage and stays,
cohesion needed for structure;
they tighten nuts & carve us
in that image, with unnamed
tentacled monsters far from the sea
and the whump, stubbornly staid,
starts almost perpetual motion,
wildness is no longer tolerated.

Cross-legged

we are, so limboed in the high
phen and all the lowly below
in the pen they follow their line
across the fell and those fallen
between lies and egos and I am
a small figure sat in a foreign land
offering you nothing from my
upturned palm, if you have received
this message in error, please notify
the sender immediately, then delete
wording must be kept in a safe
agree or we will suspend thee &

half-witted wait.

Now

these utterances mean zilch
the party huffs and puffs,
its leaders all for cover-up
feeling furrowed into muck
speak, be beaten blind, tear up
the heads of all tyrants roll,
splintering luxury, you troll
not so easy, the truth

is stark.

Tittle-tattle

the dot above an i is not
worth a jot, or two crossbes
but remember to cross
your t's, dot your ayes
while ancient trees fall,
without a yod even, when
unchallenged spouting
dowses roots, they're all
tattlers their yads full
it's only the you and I's
that's not, in deep maym,
fodder but not for cattle

that is.

Oahpa!

the one word that tells you where
the verb was done, there are
surprisingly few of them, where do
we have to stay at the moment,
home, inside, here, *In gille 'siste'*
èohkkát. (I don't like to sit inside.),
where can't we go, out, spatial small
paradigms allow for differentiating
illative and locative, a delimited area
or the path of movement, *Allet mana*
vuos 'sisa'. (Don't go in yet.)
(You are so far away and yet
so near.), at home there's total chaos
(Now, we have to think ahead.),
you are standing

in my way.

Savage indignation

You allow your ink to place
a unique sense of self on the words,

but we are bound together
by something more basic than selfhood,

this is proved on the pulses
it is as if a threshold has been crossed

into affect and percept, vivid sensations
such we need to strip meat from bone

and be moved by savage indignation,
but is this mere prancing, self-regarding,

or does it impel you to discharge
feelings in an act or act of speech,

the shortcomings of self admitted
into the intimacy of the work.

Move into evidence

gloved, they get out the facts
to ascertain truth, to inform
an opinion on a matter of lives
that itself is far removed
from this deliberation, whether
there was intent, not just before,
nor then, not even at the instant,
to shoe answers, bloody a void,
beyond a reasonable doubt. I move
that be introduced into evidence,
for this begot the friendless tide,
this is the book he made his own.
No objection.

It is received.

The 7.14

The 7.14, the train I always take, it
arrives empty from the depot so I

always get a seat, the interiors are
Christian Lacroix and lights ambient

lavender blue, just right for the not-
morning person who looks at

suburbs that roll by while listening
to drinking songs as the day dawns

behind the single chimney they left
up I don't know why and I'm alone

to reflect on the distance between
us, don't get me wrong, it's a long-

enough-distance one this, invariably
civil dawn already where you are.

It all seems so simple

We may think it's nothing
splash the face, beat the drum
a few words posted online
while the world's spirits slumber
in widespread shame, but
on the contrary, each message
shock the monkey, electrify
has the weight of a link, and that
matters, unforgettable, I feel
shockwave, surge of the sun
able to live reliefs of turmoil
an energised riff of epinephrine
don't know if this prompts nada,
maybe a luminous change within
never a shtum poet, but rather
get blood to flow in every cranny
and still, take the road to joy
no road without brittle ground,
nothing beautiful and true smooth.

All notes lead here

We ride past rows of cypresses
staves in the sunlight, climb

these trilled steps to clusters
of clock-towers with roof scales,

set up our stands, let us barter
we are offshoots of a staff,

rays of sound scattered in the hills,
our banter livens the twilight

we are on the road to somewhere
as mountains curve the score

of each valley, route to the hubbub,
we are prelude, adagio, coda

we are all notes but only the one.

The Glosters return

You are a lucky man, daffodils sprawl your drive
buds sticky on the trees and the seed at last
sprouts into green, resurgence begins from ground

frozen hard by the long winter; the grass needs mowing,
fish to turn black to gold, river pondweed yet
to grow, and grow old, sun streams and days are blessed.

It is wealth encrusted, walking once again that muddy track
spatted with cowpats and pig smell
cool whishing of grasses, this sod, with dewstrewn fields

in memory restored, slumber sweet roses, hide
from the starling chatter; so stand still,
blend in with the brilliance of a stream,

nothing is so splendid, you mutter, than to cry
walk, walk, to the warrior's limbs
as they fumble with the twilight, then dusk.

Let's be fishies

We splodge past shells sunken in shrimp pools
and, reeling in the wind, scramble over limpets

as light cracks out at sea, all purple and blue,
let's be those silvery dots in the deeps of shoals.

We'll have serrations and bar-like patches,
and doze, dreaming of fat bacon, draped in shagreen.

We'll have bright scarlet irises, grinning mouths
and remarkably slow breath, we'll sometimes slide

with that slimy slithery way of a shanny, but
eye bony hooks, they'll make us shiver a sudden.

Migration

The skies are the same for everyone
flocks of birds high against the setting sun
the aircraft heading into that crack of blue
those clouds are desert mountains
electric-wire ceramics makeshift gibbets

The skies are greying out the light
the desert an ancient map of the world
this picture of thirst that needs quenching
these hordes assailing the perimeter
this walk that is the return from darkness
where one life ends and another starts.

Home, sweet home

Open your eyes, a chill at your neck,
pare the gloom for intruders.
This is the burden. Papers damn them.

Hands stuck firmly behind your back,
retreat into the yard. Look, love,
he's cradling him. Open the gate.

Unfazed, you lope, flat footing
round the question do I take
no account be rendered, this
act of humanity, welcoming, mate.

Break out the firelighters. Squint.
Busy, as tracks shuffle, light up,
hands outstretched. Ask them in.

Mortuo mari

Plaintive geese in battle order
advance,
across the marsh

      apparently weightless
flying machines
that wink a red eye
at nobody in particular
as if to say

      look what we can do
avaricious fowl
stooped over a pit

   huddled, beautiful ebony
crowds at its edge
in plastic-sheeted shelters.

Purpose

May the shadow be our shadow,
let the stubborn light of ours
be filtered, this bedrock the foundation,
you choose words that were there
          but look
how every strand of humble thought
is slowly kneaded again,
makes us design each other anew.
          That's how
you learn to grow, ego to self,
and to sustain
– that trunk that binds us all –
shared purpose,
          common language.

Those who witness

You have come this far, through the trees and
     fire, you, watching over this earth, already
walked along sharp-edged borders,
     saw youth riddled by the hail and, let into
the secret too early, fade into the storm.

Death, hunger, wars, so many chapters of a book
     of inexhaustible content.

Is this not another landscape now, a semblance
     that looms out of nightfall, a divided-up
worn-out land-living world of passers-by whose
     memory is sieve-like, no dreams left, at
the end of the road.

Victorian fields

On the sands of Dunbarton school
a chapel stands, its dusty stone
topped with an early Florentine dome.

Through rhododendron bushes
tarmac paths run and weave,
among cricket whites, sunset blue.

Where children play and eat
on neat Royce tables, pray
to sainted fathers, plaques

on the wall, follow Victorian ways
where bracken straddles the bends
and the master's dogs waddle

along the colonnade, red brick arch,
playing field, and spotless grass
our college, our teens, at last.

Moon-time

The gibbous one greet me coldly,
rain squeezed me int'pub but maid
tek n'gorm. Scarpered. Blasted
slippery soles. The boots is off.

The moon-eyed peer through net,
rakers prowl the cussen gates,
addled so an' all. She scuttled,
turned back away from my shiner,

my gloved hand, fingers waiting
to catch the moon-dark when falls
from pocket, as tha moon-call

sung in square. I'm no closer, is it
not a lost cause, or no cause t'all,
cheese it, tha squinten puddle-face!

Reaching out

Things are often simpler than what we say,
when a woman very lightly leans forward
to see that light, the sun that is curtained.

The quilted bedcover, white furniture,
this sentence in the half-dark, a dialogue
to be continued silently, this instant.

This is a thought held out to someone
who is a still a stranger maybe
who seeks another realm, intact, shared.

The writer

I see the chair he sits in
the typewriter, the glare
scrawled notes & biro

I sit behind him,
as he bleeds memories
into unfinished works

I am immersed
in the conductor's music
this intelligence

He grinds himself
into each phrase, this joy
terrible isolation

I don't know which.

The lure of the sea

I slime up steps from the grey rock
then on the greenstone,

dripping figures, trampling on,
shelter from the storm. Here inside

bay windows I see slurring trees
encircled by sea-walls.

Imagine them fooling around out there
as bullseye green blurs the hexes,

our uplighters streak the spray,
horizons draw in. Tread gently,

the deep groans, such endless muttering,
the sea must let its shades go.

October in Bucharest

Skate round dirt-board stalls spread with earthy leaves, negotiate a laden porter's trolley. Trams turning disgorge shouldered sacks of apples, leave behind slick trails crossing a junction peppered with cinnamon faces. Was then. Moving targets spattered with scarlet scarves. Weather torn, moving slowly but not going nowhere, living, queuing. We are the only ones hurrying nowhere. That is then. What is this.

Cobblestones that glisten. Sidestepping black puddles & tarmac lakes, we walk among desire's ghosts, gripped by tense silence. We are that. Refracted light of a shroud in her palm, sharpened by crisp air, by midnight's shades and portals. Solitary lamps, gleaming polished silver along dark undulating curves. Watchful, the deserted street. Olive-dark steps climb beyond. What is. The tall iron-wrought gate to her winged court clanks behind. Rain falling, lightly, across her breach spread and opening. So this is what.

We want to touch.

The shoreline

We tread on the limpet-encrusted
slipway to the shallows,
rockface debris spilling into the sea
that draws in its breath.

Condensed layers of ages
behind us, mizzle on the watchtower,
the distance travelled here
shorter to the eye than that taken.

Leave footprints in sand as,
softly, like a whisper, waves reach up
clutching as they break free
sliding back, ready to have another go.

Sea and land

The cold air is billowing through the cabin
Christ the redeemer is draped in the national colours
we are disinfected when entering
the boats return to the harbour at the day's end
the man at the helm a woman still stretched out across the bow
they are being delivered and
the sea flashing gold sprinkles
and this is going nowhere
days spent thinking of nothing
but emptying the mind
and sleep
the black sand still burns my soles
the church is aflame again
mountains covered in mist and rumbling
roads winding along the coast under flowers
they're dressed in black and running at dawn
they're dressed in white and crowding
the roads at night
there are jumpers, card-players and day trip trains
this is just a litany of lives
and they all have stories to tell.

Reopening

Leaving the house in the dead of day
to go shopping in a light drizzle
in shops where assistants outnumber ten to one
in streets where all the bars are closed
and people hurry to the tube
and police stand at each corner

but the Christmas lights are still out
and the perfumes encourage one
to start thinking of presents
and real people
not just those endless faces and lives
we scroll through
day after day
just marking time
nothing more.

Subterranean explorers of words

Enter the vast passage stretching underground
    the bustling chatter
whose formation dates back millennia
        "It's just beautiful,"
the network of utterances fellow spelunkers find.
        "The words are layers of fudge;
            treacle, dark, ochre, obscure."
Researchers had long poked around known,
        alleys, suspecting more to it.
Discovered the meaning lies below.
    drilled into sub-text to access the passage
        dowse, locate equivalence,
detect anomalies of speech,
        signifying a communicant or void beyond.

Now all left was the gruelling task of
 piercing ancient idioms of parole
   drill and chisel a window through.
They got lucky when softer vowels gave way,
  "There was indeed a glottis
  wider than we thought,"
They found
 this subterranean chamber steeped in words.
  "The sense is immutable."
Massive thoughts ruptured the bedrock,
  yellow calcite encrusted the words
   plosives popping bright colour.

They crawled and waded through.
       "The words are perfectly smooth, perfectly vertical"
The course ran until their travels were stymied by incomprehension.
       "It keeps going, we have no idea where it will end"

The hope is to return when the noise recedes.
   determine exact depth and extent,
       and one day open up the aperture
     "It's a great discovery, we're very happy about that.
This doesn't happen very often in a lifetime."

Are you listening?

We have not abandoned hope   in the power
of language to conserve
     and to set things right,
this nondual awareness in the face of
                       impending
ecological destruction,

this nonduality a forceful
     world without centre
         or edge
that includes everything.

Enter and unmute,
       break down borders
    between sound
and non-sound,

    never abandon the importance
of allowing space for strangeness in intimacy,
      in which
beings can be their strange selves,
        strange strangers.

www.ingramcontent.com/pod-product-compliance
Lightning Source LLC
LaVergne TN
LVHW051512170726
843492LV00002B/900